D1013041

EXTRA Nutty

KNOCK-KNOCK JOKES for Kids

BOB PHILLIPS

Cover by Dugan Design Group, Bloomington, Minnesota

Cover photos © syagci, Chris3fer / iStockphoto

EXTRA NUTTY KNOCK-KNOCK JOKES FOR KIDS
Copyright © 2011 by Bob Phillips
Published by Harvest House Publishers
Eugene, Oregon 97402
www.harvesthousepublishers.com

ISBN 978-0-7369-3061-1

Printed in the United States of America

11 12 13 14 15 16 17 18/ BP-NI / 10 9 8 7 6 5 4 3 2 1

CONTENTS

KNOCK, KNOCK!

Knock, knock.
Who's there?
Aida.
Aida who?
Aida big pizza, and now I'm full.

Knock, knock.
Who's there?
Bustle.
Bustle who?
Bustle be picking you up for school.

Knock, knock.
Who's there?
Carmen.
Carmen who?
Carmen to my arms and give me a hug.

Knock, knock.
Who's there?
Discus.
Discus who?
Discus it with me and then I'll tell you.

Knock, knock.
Who's there?
Eiffel.
Eiffel who?
Eiffel good. I had a great night's sleep.

Knock, knock.
Who's there?
Fido.
Fido who?
Fido know how long I can wait for you to open the door.

Knock, knock.
Who's there?
Gibbon.
Gibbon who?
Gibbon me a break.

Knock, knock.
Who's there?
Hedda.
Hedda who?
My hedda hurts. Do you have an aspirin?

Knock, knock.
Who's there?
Ivan.
Ivan who?
Ivan to stop you from telling anymore knock-knock jokes.

Knock, knock.
Who's there?
Jimmy.
Jimmy who?
Jimmy your key, so I can open the door.

Knock, knock.
Who's there?
Kenya.
Kenya who?
Kenya open the door? It's cold, and I'm hungry.

Knock, knock.
Who's there?
Lois.
Lois who?
Lois man on the totem pole.

Knock, knock.
Who's there?
Madison.
Madison who?
Madison is what doctors give you when you are sick.

Knock, knock.
Who's there?
Noah.
Noah who?
Noah anybody who will open the door?

Knock, knock.
Who's there?
Olive.
Olive who?
Olive to hear new knock-knock jokes.

Knock, knock.
Who's there?
Panther.
Panther who?
Panther all dirty from playing in the mud.

Knock, knock.
Who's there?
Q-tip.
Q-tip who?
Q-tip me off on how to get you to open the door?

Knock, knock.
Who's there?
Ray.
Ray who?
No, it's hoo-ray!

Knock, knock.
Who's there?
Saul.
Saul who?
Saul these jokes are too much for me.

Knock, knock.
Who's there?
Tibet.
Tibet who?
You know, Tibet way to get in is to use your key.

Knock, knock.
Who's there?
Upton.
Upton who?
Upton now, I've enjoyed telling knock-knock jokes.

Knock, knock.
Who's there?
Vanna.
Vanna who?
Vanna make something of it?

Knock, knock.
Who's there?
Wafer.
Wafer who?
Wafer a long time, but now I'm back.

Knock, knock.
Who's there?
Xylophone.
Xylophone who?
Xylophone you when I get home.

WHO'S THERE?

Knock, knock.
Who's there?
Argo.
Argo who?
Argo down to the store for some candy.

Knock, knock.
Who's there?
Betty.
Betty who?
Betty gets sore knuckles from all that knocking.

Knock, knock.
Who's there?
Chess.
Chess who?
Chess open the door and let me in.

Knock, knock.
Who's there?
Dumbbell.
Dumbbell who?
Dumbbell wouldn't work, so I had to knock.

Knock, knock.
Who's there?
Eileen.
Eileen who?
Eileen on a crutch because I broke my foot.

Knock, knock.
Who's there?
Ferris.
Ferris who?
Ferris fair, so let me in!.

Knock, knock.
Who's there?
Gladys.
Gladys who?
Gladys not snowing.

Knock, knock.
Who's there?
Hank.
Hank who?
You're welcome.

Knock, knock.
Who's there?
Icon.
Icon who?
Icon hardly wait for you to open the door.

Knock, knock.
Who's there?
Jamaica.
Jamaica who?
Jamaica new knock-knock joke?

Knock, knock.
Who's there?
Kansas.
Kansas who?
Kansas what you put soda pop in.

Knock, knock.
Who's there?
Lattice.
Lattice who?
Lattice have a good time laughing together.

Knock, knock.
Who's there?
Major.
Major who?
Major ask, didn't I!

Knock, knock.
Who's there?
Norway.
Norway who?
Norway am I going to stand outside in the cold.

Knock, knock.
Who's there?
Olga.
Olga who?
Olga play with my friends.

Knock, knock.
Who's there?
Paradise.
Paradise who?
Paradise is what you roll when you play Monopoly.

Knock, knock.
Who's there?
Q-tip.
Q-tip who?
If Q-tip over a glass of milk, you'll make a mess.

Knock, knock.
Who's there?
Rose.
Rose who?
Rose, rose, rose your boat, gently down the stream…

Knock, knock.
Who's there?
Settler.
Settler who?
Settler down! She's acting silly again.

Knock, knock.
Who's there?
Tijuana.
Tijuana who?
Tijuana hold my hand?

Knock, knock.
Who's there?
Utah.
Utah who?
Utah me when you looked out the window.

Knock, knock.
Who's there?
Vonda.
Vonda who?
Vonda hear some more knock-knock jokes?

Knock, knock.
Who's there?
Wendy.
Wendy who?
Wendy red, red robin comes bob, bob, bobbin' along...

Knock, knock.
Who's there?
Xavier.
Xavier who?
Xavier breath.

STOP THAT KNOCKING!

Knock, knock.
Who's there?
Asp.
Asp who?
Stop asping me who's there. Just open the door and let
me in.

Knock, knock.
Who's there?
Black Panther.
Black Panther who?
Black Panther all I have to wear.

Knock, knock.
Who's there?
Candy.
Candy who?
Candy please tell someone else all these jokes?

Knock, knock.
Who's there?
Darrell.
Darrell who?
Darrell be an ice-cream cone for you if you open the door.

Knock, knock.
Who's there?
Eli.
Eli who?
Eli to me! He really knows who's there.

Knock, knock.
Who's there?
Franz.
Franz who?
Franz, Romans, countrymen, lend me your ears…

Knock, knock.
Who's there?
Gopher.
Gopher who?
Gopher a walk around the block?

Knock, knock.
Who's there?
Heaven.
Heaven who?
Heaven you got any idea?

Knock, knock.
Who's there?
Icon.
Icon who?
Icon give you a big hug.

Knock, knock.
Who's there?
Juneau.
Juneau who?
Juneau any more knock-knock jokes?

Knock, knock.
Who's there?
Ken.
Ken who?
Ken you come out and play?

Knock, knock.
Who's there?
Lion.
Lion who?
Lion down in the wet grass will get your shirt all wet.

Knock, knock.
Who's there?
Mega.
Mega who?
Mega me an apple pie.

Knock, knock.
Who's there?
Noun.
Noun who?
Noun is the time to open the door.

Knock, knock.
Who's there?
Olive.
Olive who?
Olive on the other side of the street.

Knock, knock.
Who's there?
Parka.
Parka who?
Parka your bike next to the tree on the front lawn.

Knock, knock.
Who's there?
Quacker.
Quacker who?
Quacker cwumbs are messes that ducks make.

Knock, knock.
Who's there?
Rubber Duck.
Rubber Duck who?
Rubber Duck dub, three men in a tub...

Knock, knock.
Who's there?
Sadie.
Sadie who?
Sadie magic word, and I'll tell you who I am.

Knock, knock.
Who's there?
Tire.
Tire who?
Tire shoestrings before you trip and fall.

Knock, knock.
Who's there?
Ugo.
Ugo who?
Ugo open the door and see.

Knock, knock.
Who's there?
Vent.
Vent who?
I vent to school this morning. What did you do?

Knock, knock.
Who's there?
Winnie.
Winnie who?
Winnie funnier joke comes along, I'll tell it.

Knock, knock.
Who's there?
Xavier.
Xavier who?
Xavier! She's sinking in the sea!

OPEN THE DOOR!

Knock, knock.
Who's there?
Avery.
Avery who?
Avery Thanksgiving I eat a lot of turkey.

Knock, knock.
Who's there?
Bean.
Bean who?
Bean standing out here for a long time.

Knock, knock.
Who's there?
Canteloupe.
Canteloupe who?
Canteloupe without a girlfriend.

Knock, knock.
Who's there?
Dewayne.
Dewayne who?
Dewayne fell on Noah's Ark for forty days and forty
    nights.

Knock, knock.
Who's there?
Elvis.
Elvis who?
Elvis help Santa at Christmastime.

Knock, knock.
Who's there?
Freddie.
Freddie who?
Freddie or not, here I come!

Knock, knock.
Who's there?
Gopher.
Gopher who?
Gopher-ther with these jokes, and I'll leave!

Knock, knock.
Who's there?
Halibut.
Halibut who?
Halibut opening the door? I'm tired of knocking.

Knock, knock.
Who's there?
Iguana.
Iguana who?
Iguana hold your hand.

Knock, knock.
Who's there?
Justin.
Justin who?
Justin time to open the door. It's cold outside.

Knock, knock.
Who's there?
Keith.
Keith who?
Keith me on the lips, sweetheart.

Knock, knock.
Who's there?
Lazy.
Lazy who?
Lazy key on the table where I can find it.

Knock, knock.
Who's there?
Megan.
Megan who?
Megan a funny joke is what I like to do.

Knock, knock.
Who's there?
Nuisance.
Nuisance who?
What's nuisance I've been gone?

Knock, knock.
Who's there?
Oliver.
Oliver who?
Oliver town, people are laughing at my knock-knock
jokes.

Knock, knock.
Who's there?
Papa.
Papa who?
Papa goes the weasel!

Knock, knock.
Who's there?
Quack.
Quack who?
Quack my tooth on a popcorn kernel.

Knock, knock.
Who's there?
Ray.
Ray who?
Ray-ders of the Lost Ark!

Knock, knock.
Who's there?
Sal.
Sal who?
Sal long way from California to New York.

Knock, knock.
Who's there?
Taiwan.
Taiwan who?
Taiwan to hear another knock-knock joke?

Knock, knock.
Who's there?
Uruguay.
Uruguay who?
You go Uruguay, and I'll go mine!

Knock, knock.
Who's there?
Veal.
Veal who?
Veal see you later.

Knock, knock.
Who's there?
Wooden shoe.
Wooden shoe who?
Wooden shoe like to hear another joke?

Knock, knock.
Who's there?
Yawl.
Yawl who?
Yawl come back and visit again.

Knock, knock.
Who's there?
Herring.
Herring who?
Herring aids can help you hear what others are saying.

Knock, knock.
Who's there?
Imus.
Imus who?
Imus be out of my mind to stay out here.

Knock, knock.
Who's there?
Jester.
Jester who?
Jester minute! I'm going to cry if you don't open the
    door.

Knock, knock.
Who's there?
Kipper.
Kipper who?
Kipper locked up in the zoo for people to look at.

Knock, knock.
Who's there?
Lecture.
Lecture who?
Lecture smile be your first hello.

Knock, knock.
Who's there?
Mummy.
Mummy who?
It takes mummy to buy a car.

Knock, knock.
Who's there?
Noah.
Noah who?
Noah good restaurant in this area?

Knock, knock.
Who's there?
Oman.
Oman who?
Oman, it's cold out here!

Knock, knock.
Who's there?
Paris.
Paris who?
Paris the thought of another knock-knock joke!

Knock, knock.
Who's there?
Quark, quark, quark!
Quark, quark, quark who?
Are you a duck?

Knock, knock.
Who's there?
Ray.
Ray who?
Ray-member me?

Knock, knock.
Who's there?
Salami.
Salami who?
Salami in already!

Knock, knock.
Who's there?
Tally.
Tally who?
Are you from England?

Knock, knock.
Who's there?
Usher.
Usher who?
Usher wish you would let me in!

Knock, knock.
Who's there?
Venice.
Venice who?
Venice it time to open the door?

Knock, knock.
Who's there?
William.
William who?
William mind bringing me an ice-cream cone?

Knock, knock.
Who's there?
Yoga.
Yoga who?
Yoga any idea how tired I am of all these jokes?

LeT Me IN!

Knock, knock.
Who's there?
Alpaca.
Alpaca who?
Alpaca my bags and leave if you don't let me in.

Knock, knock.
Who's there?
Bandage.
Bandage who?
Bandage is determining how long a band has been
    playing.

Knock, knock.
Who's there?
Cauliflower.
Cauliflower who?
Cauliflower whatever you want–it's still a flower.

Knock, knock.
Who's there?
Donut.
Donut who?
A donut is a weird person who only eats dough.

Knock, knock.
Who's there?
Esther.
Esther who?
Esther anybody who will answer the door?

Knock, knock.
Who's there?
Fresno.
Fresno who?
Rudolf the Fresno reindeer.

Knock, knock.
Who's there?
Gophers.
Gophers who?
Gophers to the store, second to the library, and third to
    Grandma's.

Knock, knock.
Who's there?
Howie.
Howie who?
I'm fine. How are you?

Knock, knock.
Who's there?
Iona.
Iona who?
Iona new car. Want to go for a ride?

Knock, knock.
Who's there?
Justice.
Justice who?
Justice the best kind of judge to have when you go to
    court.

Knock, knock.
Who's there?
Kipper.
Kipper who?
Kipper silly knock-knock jokes to yourself.

Knock, knock.
Who's there?
Leena.
Leena who?
Leena too far over the wall, and you'll fall over.

Knock, knock.
Who's there?
Mabel.
Mabel who?
Mabel go knock on someone else's door.

Knock, knock.
Who's there?
New Year.
New Year who?
New Year gonna ask me that!

Knock, knock.
Who's there?
Orbit.
Orbit who?
Orbit of a strange person.

Knock, knock.
Who's there?
Paris.
Paris who?
A Paris good, but I prefer apples!

Knock, knock.
Who's there?
Quebec.
Quebec who?
Quebec to the end of the line!

Knock, knock.
Who's there?
Racine.
Racine who?
Racine around in circles all day?

Knock, knock.
Who's there?
Sally.
Sally who?
Sally-brate the moments of your life!

Knock, knock.
Who's there?
Tanks.
Tanks who?
Tanks for opening the door.

Knock, knock.
Who's there?
Uta.
Uta who?
Uta sight, uta mind!

Knock, knock.
Who's there?
Venue.
Venue who?
Venue stop telling knock-knock jokes, I'll be glad.

Knock, knock.
Who's there?
Wales.
Wales who?
Wales long as I'm here, shall we go out?

Knock, knock.
Who's there?
Yancy.
Yancy who?
Yancy meeting you here!

WHO'S BANGING ON THE DOOR?

Knock, knock.
Who's there?
Alpha.
Alpha who?
Alpha crying out loud! Please open the door!

Knock, knock.
Who's there?
Biplane.
Biplane who?
Biplane is the way I'm going home if you don't open
the door.

Knock, knock.
Who's there?
Cauliflower.
Cauliflower who?
Cauliflower if you want a date with a daisy.

Knock, knock.
Who's there?
Denial.
Denial who?
Denial is a river in Egypt.

Knock, knock.
Who's there?
Esther.
Esther who?
Esther another way to get you to open the door besides
knocking?

Knock, knock.
Who's there?
Felice.
Felice who?
Felice a jolly good fellow…which nobody can deny.

Knock, knock.
Who's there?
Gomez.
Gomez who?
Gomez around with me, buddy.

Knock, knock.
Who's there?
Hertz.
Hertz who?
Hertz me when you won't let me in.

Knock, knock.
Who's there?
Iowa.
Iowa who?
Iowa lotta money to the IRS.

Knock, knock.
Who's there?
Jackson.
Jackson who?
Jackson is also the son of Jack's wife.

Knock, knock.
Who's there?
Kumquat.
Kumquat who?
Kumquat-ly while they take you away to the loony farm.

Knock, knock.
Who's there?
Les.
Les who?
Les go to the party.

Knock, knock.
Who's there?
Mistake.
Mistake who?
Mistake was just put on the barbeque.

Knock, knock.
Who's there?
Nana.
Nana who?
Nana your business.

Knock, knock.
Who's there?
Ooze.
Ooze who?
Ooze in charge around here?

Knock, knock.
Who's there?
Paris.
Paris who?
Paris the salt, please!

Knock, knock.
Who's there?
Quack.
Quack who?
Quack an egg and fry it in the skillet.

Knock, knock.
Who's there?
Raisin.
Raisin who?
Raisin kids is not easy.

Knock, knock.
Who's there?
Sally.
Sally who?
Sally dance while the music is playing?

Knock, knock.
Who's there?
Tennis.
Tennis who?
Tennis just before eleven.

Knock, knock.
Who's there?
Undo.
Undo who?
Undo-wear is what I put on first.

Knock, knock.
Who's there?
Vera.
Vera who?
Vera funny–now open the door!

Knock, knock.
Who's there?
Waiter.
Waiter who?
Waiter minute while I tie my shoelaces!

Knock, knock.
Who's there?
Yankee.
Yankee who?
Yankee-doodle-do, that's who!

I HEAR A RAPPING SOUND!

Knock, knock.
Who's there?
Amahl.
Amahl who?
Amahl is where I like to go shopping.

Knock, knock.
Who's there?
Balls.
Balls who?
Balls well that ends well.

Knock, knock.
Who's there?
Cauliflower.
Cauliflower who?
Cauliflower and I'll call you crazy.

Knock, knock.
Who's there?
Disaster.
Disaster who?
Disaster be the worst knock-knock joke I've ever heard.

Knock, knock.
Who's there?
Eliza.
Eliza who?
Eliza lot, so you can't trust him.

Knock, knock.
Who's there?
Furs.
Furs who?
Furs you sit down, and then you put on your socks and
    shoes.

Knock, knock.
Who's there?
Gull.
Gull who?
Gulls like to go shopping at the mall.

Knock, knock.
Who's there?
Hobbit.
Hobbit who?
Hobbit opening the door?

Knock, knock.
Who's there?
Ivana.
Ivana who?
Ivana come in! Open the door!

Knock, knock.
Who's there?
Joust.
Joust who?
Joust about time for dinner.

Knock, knock.
Who's there?
Kai.
Kai who?
My Kai flies in the sky on windy days.

Knock, knock.
Who's there?
Lego.
Lego who?
Lego of the door handle.

Knock, knock.
Who's there?
Mississippi.
Mississippi who?
Mississippi is Mr. Ippi's wife.

Knock, knock.
Who's there?
Nero.
Nero who?
Nero far, you're still my best friend.

Knock, knock.
Who's there?
Orange.
Orange who?
Orange you tired of all these knock-knock jokes?

Knock, knock.
Who's there?
Pasta.
Pasta who?
Pasta peanut butter sandwich, please.

Knock, knock.
Who's there?
Queen.
Queen who?
Queen up this porch. It's a mess!

Knock, knock.
Who's there?
Rice.
Rice who?
Rice up early in the morning.

Knock, knock.
Who's there?
Sam.
Sam who?
Sam enchanted evening…

Knock, knock.
Who's there?
Tex.
Tex who?
Tex messages can be sent on your cell phone.

Knock, knock.
Who's there?
Urania.
Urania who?
Urania my parade, and that doesn't make me happy.

Knock, knock.
Who's there?
Viper.
Viper who?
Viper the windows. They're dirty.

Knock, knock.
Who's there?
William Tell.
William Tell who?
William, Tell your mother to come to the door.

Knock, knock.
Who's there?
Yoke.
Yoke who?
The yoke's on you! Ha!

WHO'S HAMMERING ON THE DOOR?

Knock, knock.
Who's there?
A Mayan.
A Mayan who?
A Mayan the wrong porch, knocking on the wrong door?

Knock, knock.
Who's there?
Balls.
Balls who?
Balls fair in love and war.

Knock, knock.
Who's there?
Coconut.
Coconut who?
Coconut is a person who drinks cocoa every chance he
    gets.

Knock, knock.
Who's there?
Donahue.
Donahue who?
Donahue want to know who is standing outside knocking on your door?

Knock, knock.
Who's there?
Eel.
Eel who?
Eel is what your broken bones do when the doctor puts them in a cast.

Knock, knock.
Who's there?
France.
France who?
My France and I play ball during recess.

Knock, knock.
Who's there?
Gallop.
Gallop who?
Gallop down some soda pop with me.

Knock, knock.
Who's there?
Honeydew.
Honeydew who?
Honeydew you love me?

Knock, knock.
Who's there?
Izzy.
Izzy who?
Izzy come, izzy go.

Knock, knock.
Who's there?
Juana.
Juana who?
Juana go for a walk?

Knock, knock.
Who's there?
Kenya.
Kenya who?
Kenya get me a drink? I'm thirsty.

Knock, knock.
Who's there?
Lewis.
Lewis who?
Lewis and Clark were explorers.

Knock, knock.
Who's there?
Marcus.
Marcus who?
Marcus waiting for you to come out and play.

Knock, knock.
Who's there?
Newton.
Newton who?
Newton had an apple fall on his head.

Knock, knock.
Who's there?
Olive.
Olive who?
Olive and let live.

Knock, knock.
Who's there?
Pig.
Pig who?
Pig up your stuff and put it away.

Knock, knock.
Who's there?
Queen.
Queen who?
Sour queen is what I like on potatoes!

Knock, knock.
Who's there?
Roach.
Roach who?
Roach you a letter. Did you get it?

Knock, knock.
Who's there?
Salmon.
Salmon who?
Salmon Ella have been married for 50 years.

Knock, knock.
Who's there?
Therese.
Therese who?
Therese got to be an end to these crazy jokes.

Knock, knock.
Who's there?
Unaware.
Unaware who?
Unaware is what you don't answer the door in.

Knock, knock.
Who's there?
Venda.
Venda who?
Venda knocks keep coming, you'll open the door.

Knock, knock.
Who's there?
Who.
Who who?
You sound like an owl.
Knock, knock.

Who's there?
Yule.
Yule who?
Yule be glad this is almost the last joke.

KNOCK IT OFF!

Knock, knock.
Who's there?
Amish.
Amish who?
Amish you a whole lot.

Knock, knock.
Who's there?
Burton.
Burton who?
Burton the hand is worth two in the bush.

Knock, knock.
Who's there?
Chester.
Chester who?
Chester minute! I'm on the telephone.

Knock, knock.
Who's there?
Dewey.
Dewey who?
Dewey have any way to stop telling knock-knock jokes?

Knock, knock.
Who's there?
Ellen.
Ellen who?
Ellen you my bicycle if you promise to bring it back.

Knock, knock.
Who's there?
Foyer.
Foyer who?
Foyer information, it's Spider-Man.

Knock, knock.
Who's there?
Ghana.
Ghana who?
Ghana keep knocking till you open this door!

Knock, knock.
Who's there?
Hiram.
Hiram who?
Hiram tired of all these silly jokes.

Knock, knock.
Who's there?
Igor.
Igor who?
Igor to come inside if you ever open the door.

Knock, knock.
Who's there?
Juicy.
Juicy who?
Juicy the flying saucer?

Knock, knock.
Who's there?
Ketchup.
Ketchup who?
Ketchup with me if you can.

Knock, knock.
Who's there?
License.
License who?
He didn't license the last time.

Knock, knock.
Who's there?
Midas.
Midas who?
Midas well tell you another knock-knock joke.

Knock, knock.
Who's there?
Niacin.
Niacin who?
Niacin quiet around here, isn't it?

Knock, knock.
Who's there?
Ostrich.
Ostrich who?
Ostrich my arms when I wake up in the morning.

Knock, knock.
Who's there?
Pizza.
Pizza who?
Pizza cake would sure taste good right now.

Knock, knock.
Who's there?
Queen.
Queen who?
Queen and tidy, that's how your room should be kept.

Knock, knock.
Who's there?
Rocco.
Rocco who?
Rocco roll is my favorite kind of music.

Knock, knock.
Who's there?
Samoa.
Samoa who?
Samoa ice cream, please.

Knock, knock.
Who's there?
Thomas.
Thomas who?
Thomas is a bunch of toes.

Knock, knock.
Who's there?
Uneeda.
Uneeda who?
Uneeda brush your teeth.

Knock, knock.
Who's there?
Vera.
Vera who?
I'm Vera tired of these nutty knock-knock jokes.

Knock, knock.
Who's there?
Warrior.
Warrior who?
Warrior been all of my life?

Knock, knock.
Who's there?
Yucatan.
Yucatan who?
Yucatan very fast and even get sunburned without sun-
   tan lotion.

STOP THAT NOISE!

Knock, knock.
Who's there?
Amoeba.
Amoeba who?
Amoeba silly, but I like knock-knock jokes.

Knock, knock.
Who's there?
Boo-hoo.
Boo-hoo who?
Boo-hoo-hoo.
Boo-hoo-hoo who?
Boo-hoo-hoo-hoo.
Boo-hoo-hoo-hoo who?
Boo-hoo-hoo-hoo-hoo.
Boo-hoo-hoo-hoo-hoo who?
Stop it! You're breaking my heart.

Knock, knock.
Who's there?
Camel.
Camel who?
Camel come out and play?

Knock, knock.
Who's there?
Dinosaur.
Dinosaur who?
Dinosaur because she stubbed her toe.

Knock, knock.
Who's there?
Emerson.
Emerson who?
Emerson funny knock-knock jokes.

Knock, knock.
Who's there?
Five.
Five who?
Five been out here knocking for a long time.

Knock, knock.
Who's there?
Gwen.
Gwen who?
Gwen you stop telling knock-knock jokes, I'll be very
    happy.

Knock, knock.
Who's there?
Howard.
Howard who?
Howard you like to go to Disneyland?

Knock, knock.
Who's there?
Irish.
Irish who?
Irish I knew.

Knock, knock.
Who's there?
Just Ashen.
Just Ashen who?
Just Ashen if anyone will let me in.

Knock, knock.
Who's there?
Kleenex.
Kleenex who?
Kleenex I've ever been is after I take a bath.

Knock, knock.
Who's there?
Leif.
Leif who?
Leifs are what grow on trees.

Knock, knock.
Who's there?
Macaw.
Macaw who?
Macaw ran out of gas.

Knock, knock.
Who's there?
Noah.
Noah who?
Noah good knock-knock joke?

Knock, knock.
Who's there?
Oliver.
Oliver who?
Oliver is what people who like liver say before they eat it.

Knock, knock.
Who's there?
Police.
Police who?
Police give me a candy bar.

Knock, knock.
Who's there?
Quiet.
Quiet who?
Quiet a long ride to the ocean, isn't it?

Knock, knock.
Who's there?
Roland.
Roland who?
Roland on the river.

Knock, knock.
Who's there?
Seahorse.
Seahorse who?
Seahorse around and you always get in trouble.

Knock, knock.
Who's there?
Tyler.
Tyler who?
Tyler is someone who lays tiles on the floor.

Knock, knock.
Who's there?
Upton.
Upton who?
It's Upton you to open the door.

Knock, knock.
Who's there?
Vine.
Vine who?
Vine weather to go swimming.
Knock, knock.

Who's there?
Wa.
Wa who?
Hey, are you a cowboy?

Knock, knock.
Who's there?
You.
You who?
You who to you too.

THE DOOR IS SHUT!

Knock, knock.
Who's there?
Amos.
Amos who?
Amos be bugging you a lot.

Knock, knock.
Who's there?
Basket.
Basket who?
Basket home because it's nearly dark!

Knock, knock.
Who's there?
Canter.
Canter who?
Canter you come out and go for a bike ride?

Knock, knock.
Who's there?
Delight.
Delight who?
Delight on your porch burnt my finger.

Knock, knock.
Who's there?
Essay.
Essay who?
Essay for you to say.

Knock, knock.
Who's there?
Fiddle.
Fiddle who?
Fiddle secrets are hard to keep.

Knock, knock.
Who's there?
G.I.
G.I. who?
G.I. wish you would give me ten dollars.

Knock, knock.
Who's there?
Hugh.
Hugh who?
Hugh da man!

Knock, knock.
Who's there?
Ida.
Ida who?
Ida like to come inside.

Knock, knock.
Who's there?
Juneau.
Juneau who?
Juneau anything besides knock-knock jokes?

Knock, knock.
Who's there?
Kuwait.
Kuwait who?
Kuwait till I tie my shoe?

Knock, knock.
Who's there?
Lena.
Lena who?
Lena against the door is tiresome, so open up!

Knock, knock.
Who's there?
Mackie.
Mackie who?
Mackie-roni and cheese is my favorite lunch.

Knock, knock.
Who's there?
Noah.
Noah who?
Noah business like show business.

Knock, knock.
Who's there?
Oil.
Oil who?
Oil see you later, alligator.

Knock, knock.
Who's there?
Police.
Police who?
Police, give me a break.

Knock, knock.
Who's there?
Quill.
Quill who?
Quill you ever stop telling these wacky jokes?

Knock, knock.
Who's there?
Rapture.
Rapture who?
Rapture presents for Christmas.

Knock, knock.
Who's there?
Saul.
Saul who?
Saul these jokes are driving me crazy.

Knock, knock.
Who's there?
Thistle.
Thistle who?
Thistle make you laugh.

Knock, knock.
Who's there?
Van Nuys.
Van Nuys who?
Van Nuys have seen the glory…

Knock, knock.
Who's there?
Wade.
Wade who?
Wade in the water and get wet.

Knock, knock.
Who's there?
Yolanda.
Yolanda who?
Yolanda your back when you slip on a banana peel.

HOLD YOUR HORSES!

Knock, knock.
Who's there?
Ancient.
Ancient who?
Ancient going to let me in?

Knock, knock.
Who's there?
Bass.
Bass who?
Bass the salt and pepper, please.

Knock, knock.
Who's there?
Cameron.
Cameron who?
Cameron is what I take pictures with.

Knock, knock.
Who's there?
Domino.
Domino who?
Domino cowhand from the Rio Grande.

Knock, knock.
Who's there?
Esther.
Esther who?
Esther anybody home?

Knock, knock.
Who's there?
Fay Row.
Fay Row who?
Fay Row was buried in a pyramid.

Knock, knock.
Who's there?
Galahad.
Galahad who?
Galahad a bike until it was stolen.

Knock, knock.
Who's there?
Hewlett.
Hewlett who?
Hewlett the cat in the house?

Knock, knock.
Who's there?
Ida Mann.
Ida Mann who?
Ida Mann who should be let in.

Knock, knock.
Who's there?
Juno.
Juno who?
Juno anyone who will open this door?

Knock, knock.
Who's there?
Ken.
Ken who?
Ken you stop telling these knock-knock jokes?

Knock, knock.
Who's there?
Lenny.
Lenny who?
Lenny body home?

Knock, knock.
Who's there?
Major.
Major who?
Major come to the door.

Knock, knock.
Who's there?
Noah.
Noah who?
Noah fence, but I'm not going to tell you.

Knock, knock.
Who's there?
Oink-oink.
Oink-oink who?
Let me guess. You're part pig and part owl.

Knock, knock.
Who's there?
Pear.
Pear who?
Pear-haps you'll stop telling silly jokes.

Knock, knock.
Who's there?
Quick.
Quick who?
Quick telling me these jokes.

Knock, knock.
Who's there?
Ray.
Ray who?
That's what a backward cheerleader shouts.

Knock, knock.
Who's there?
Sawyer.
Sawyer who?
Sawyer picture on a wanted poster.

Knock, knock.
Who's there?
Theophilus.
Theophilus who?
Theophilus knock-knock jokes I've ever heard are these ones!

Knock, knock.
Who's there?
Vonce.
Vonce who?
Vonce in a while I come up with a new knock-knock joke.

Knock, knock.
Who's there?
Wanda.
Wanda who?
Wanda hold my hand?

Knock, knock.
Who's there?
Yoda.
Yoda who?
Yoda funniest person I've ever known.

I'M NOT OPENING THE DOOR!

Knock, knock.
Who's there?
Andy.
Andy who?
Andy-lay another minute and I'm going to go home!

Knock, knock.
Who's there?
Byron.
Byron who?
Don't just Byron joke book. There are many more
     where this one came from.

Knock, knock.
Who's there?
Carson.
Carson who?
Carson the garage with the door shut.
Knock, knock.

Who's there?
Dozen.
Dozen who?
Dozen anybody want to open the door?

Knock, knock.
Who's there?
E.T.
E.T. who?
E.T. too much food, and you'll get fat.

Knock, knock.
Who's there?
Few.
Few who?
Few only knew, you would not keep me outside.

Knock, knock.
Who's there?
Ghosts go.
Ghosts go who?
No, no, you silly. Ghosts go "boo."
Knock, knock.

Who's there?
Harley.
Harley who?
Harley hear ya! Can ya speak up?

Knock, knock.
Who's there?
Ida.
Ida who?
Ida rather be inside. It's cold out here!

Knock, knock.
Who's there?
July.
July who?
July too much, and people don't believe you.

Knock, knock.
Who's there?
Kent.
Kent who?
Kent you see? I'm standing right in front of you.
Knock, knock.

Who's there?
Lesson.
Lesson who?
In lesson a minute, I'm going to leave.

Knock, knock.
Who's there?
Marmalade.
Marmalade who?
Marmalade an egg, but Papa didn't.

Knock, knock.
Who's there?
Noah.
Noah who?
Noah more of these knock-knock jokes, please!

Knock, knock.
Who's there?
Olaf.
Olaf who?
Olaf out loud at all of these jokes.
Knock, knock.

Who's there?
Pecan.
Pecan who?
Pecan someone your own size.

Knock, knock.
Who's there?
Quark.
Quark who?
Quark hard at your job, and you'll go far.

Knock, knock.
Who's there?
Razor.
Razor who?
Razor window and talk with me.

Knock, knock.
Who's there?
Scold.
Scold who?
Scold out here. Let me in!
Knock, knock.

Who's there?
Turnip.
Turnip who?
Turnip the music. I can't hear it!

Knock, knock.
Who's there?
Venus.
Venus who?
Venus it time to stop telling knock-knock jokes?

Knock, knock.
Who's there?
Warner.
Warner who?
Warner hear another knock-knock joke?

Knock, knock.
Who's there?
You.
You who?
Did you call me?

WHO'S BEATING THE DOOR DOWN?

Knock, knock.
Who's there?
Abyssinia.
Abyssinia who?
Abyssinia after a while, crocodile.

Knock, knock.
Who's there?
Basis.
Basis who?
Basis are what you run to in baseball.

Knock, knock.
Who's there?
Celeste.
Celeste who?
Celeste time I'm going to tell you a knock-knock joke.

Knock, knock.
Who's there?
Dewey.
Dewey who?
Dewey have any new knock-knock jokes? I'm getting
tired of these!

Knock, knock.
Who's there?
Eubie.
Eubie who?
Eubie a funny-looking person.

Knock, knock.
Who's there?
Fashion.
Fashion who?
Fashion your helmet in case you fall off of your bike.

Knock, knock.
Who's there?
Goblin.
Goblin who?
Goblin down your food is not very polite.

Knock, knock.
Who's there?
Hero.
Hero who?
Hero, row, row your boat gently down the stream.

Knock, knock.
Who's there?
I am.
I am who?
You mean you don't know who you are?

Knock, knock.
Who's there?
Jenelle.
Jenelle who?
Jenelle the picture of Spider-Man on the wall?

Knock, knock.
Who's there?
Kansas.
Kansas who?
Kansas be possible that you're going to open the door?

Knock, knock.
Who's there?
Lizard.
Lizard who?
Lizard that you wanted me to come over to your house, and so here I am.

Knock, knock.
Who's there?
Maya.
Maya who?
Maya good storyteller?

Knock, knock.
Who's there?
Noah.
Noah who?
Noah more knock-knock jokes if you just let me in.

Knock, knock.
Who's there?
Oliver.
Oliver who?
Oliver friends went home. She's the only one still knocking.

Knock, knock.
Who's there?
Pepper.
Pepper who?
Pepper makes me sneeze.

Knock, knock.
Who's there?
Quiche.
Quiche who?
Quiche me, and I'll quiche you.

Knock, knock.
Who's there?
Rhino.
Rhino who?
Rhino a lot. How much do you know?

Knock, knock.
Who's there?
Scott.
Scott who?
Scott a lot more of these jokes. Do you want to hear
    them?

Knock, knock.
Who's there?
Tree.
Tree who?
Tree more days till Christmas.

Knock, knock.
Who's there?
Viola.
Viola who?
Viola sudden you don't know me?

Knock, knock.
Who's there?
Wet.
Wet who?
Wet me tell you a funny story.

Knock, knock.
Who's there?
Ya.
Ya who?
It sounds like you're happy.

USe THe DOORBeLL!

Knock, knock.
Who's there?
Anita.
Anita who?
Anita someone to open the door.

Knock, knock.
Who's there?
Bayou.
Bayou who?
Did you make up these jokes bayou self?

Knock, knock.
Who's there?
Chicken.
Chicken who?
Chicken to see if you are awake.

Knock, knock.
Who's there?
Diesel.
Diesel who?
Diesel be a funny joke.

Knock, knock.
Who's there?
Europe.
Europe who?
Europe early this morning, aren't you?

Knock, knock.
Who's there?
Fido.
Fido who?
Fido known you weren't going to open the door, I
    wouldn't have come over.

Knock, knock.
Who's there?
Grouper.
Grouper who?
Grouper is a pretty fishy name.

Knock, knock.
Who's there?
Hera.
Hera who?
Hera new knock-knock joke lately?

Knock, knock.
Who's there?
Ivan.
Ivan who?
Ivan to go get a hamburger.

Knock, knock.
Who's there?
Jackal.
Jackal who?
Jackal get in if he has a key.

Knock, knock.
Who's there?
Katie.
Katie who?
Katie is for people whose names start with K and like
    to drink tea.

Knock, knock.
Who's there?
Lisa.
Lisa who?
To Lisa car costs lots of money.

Knock, knock.
Who's there?
Myth.
Myth who?
I myth my two fwont teeth.

Knock, knock.
Who's there?
Nadia.
Nadia who?
Nadia head if you like knock-knock jokes.

Knock, knock.
Who's there?
Odessa.
Odessa who?
Odessa funny joke.

Knock, knock.
Who's there?
Pest.
Pest who?
Pest the dessert, please. Cake's my favorite!

Knock, knock.
Who's there?
Queen.
Queen who?
Queen up the dirty dishes.

Knock, knock.
Who's there?
Rhoda.
Rhoda who?
Rhoda round the block a few times.

Knock, knock.
Who's there?
Shellfish.
Shellfish who?
Shellfish people think only about themselves and won't
    answer the door.

Knock, knock.
Who's there?
Toucan.
Toucan who?
Toucan have a good time playing catch.

Knock, knock.
Who's there?
Vanda.
Vanda who?
Vanda come outside and play ball?

Knock, knock.
Who's there?
Warrior.
Warrior who?
Warrior been? I've been knocking on this door all day!

Knock, knock.
Who's there?
Yvonne.
Yvonne who?
Yvonne you will get tired of all these jokes.

Harvest House Books
by Bob Phillips

For more information, send a self-addressed
stamped envelope to

Family Services
P.O. Box 9363
Fresno, California 93702